Personal Accounts

INVOLVING DISABLED CHILDREN IN RESEARCH

Bryony Beresford

SOCIAL POLICY RESEARCH UNIT

© Social Policy Research Unit 1997
Applications for reproduction should be made in writing to The Stationery
Office Limited, St Crispins, Duke Street, Norwich NR3 1PD
First published 1997

ISBN 0 11 702148 2

SPRU Editorial Group:
Sally Baldwin
Anne Corden
Lorna Foster
Jane Lightfoot
Patricia Sloper

Editor for this paper: Patricia Sloper

British Library Cataloguing in Publication Data

Printed in the United Kingdom for The Stationery Office.
Dd.303559, 2/97, C8, 3396/4, 5673, 364240.

Acknowledgements

The work involved in carrying out this review was funded by the Northern and Yorkshire Regional Health Authority.

A number of people gave advice and help while I researched and wrote this review. In particular, I would like to thank Carol Robinson and Jennifer Lauroul from the Norah Fry Research Centre for the time they gave talking to me about their experiences of research with disabled children. I am also very grateful for the support of my colleagues, Sally Baldwin and Tricia Sloper, and their contributions to the review when it was being redrafted to produce this book. Finally, my thanks go to Lorna Foster for her meticulous editorial work, and to Jenny Bowes and Teresa Frank for typing the manuscript.

Contents

Introduction

Research on childhood disability which has sought the views of the children themselves has been exceedingly rare in the past (Ward, 1997). There is now a growing conviction that, in the future, research about disability in childhood must seek to understand the child's experience and to obtain the views and opinions of the children themselves. Such a commitment is both admirable and long overdue. However, it is vital that disabled children who *are* involved in research find it a positive and helpful experience. This means that issues related to research design, methods and ethics need to be carefully considered. In response to these concerns, and as preparation for a programme of research which will be seeking children's views, the Social Policy Research Unit obtained funding from the Northern and Yorkshire Health Authority to carry out a literature review of research techniques used to obtain the views of disabled children and young people. This publication is the culmination of that review.

Disabled children are doubly disadvantaged when it comes to having the opportunity to express their views and concerns in research. Methodological and ethical arguments, together with a simple failure to accept the value of the child's viewpoint, have precluded children in general from being accepted as *bona fide* participants in research. Having an impairment, or illness, marginalises some children even further. So, in order to explore issues related to research with disabled children fully, two quite distinct bodies of literature need to be covered. The first concerns research with children *per se*, and the second, research on childhood disability. Within this latter field, studies which have consulted disabled children (of which there are very few) tend to occur within the paediatric literature. Hence, a wide body of research and discussion papers from a number of disciplines has been consulted in the course of carrying out the review; this rather diverse body of literature is reviewed and discussed in a sequence of sections which seek to take the reader from a consideration of broad policy, theoretical and ethical considerations to the pragmatics of doing research with disabled children. Since disabled children are a very heterogeneous group – in terms of age, impairment and culture, among other things – care has been taken to incorporate the impact of such factors into the discussion as far as possible.

In Chapter Two we begin the review by outlining the reasons why children *should* be involved in research, why this has not happened in the past and how current policy developments are prompting a shift. Chapter Three moves on to consider the type of approach which is appropriate for research with disabled children. Chapter Four explores the differences between adults and children, and the implications of these differences for research design. Chapter Five discusses ways of addressing the ethical issues raised by research with children. Chapter Six takes a closer look at particular research techniques using, where possible, examples from research with disabled children and young children. Chapter Seven considers how these techniques can be applied or modified when working with children with learning or communication difficulties. Chapter Eight describes ways of increasing the involvement of children in the whole research process. In concluding comments, Chapter Nine highlights the importance of finding methods to involve children truly in research.

Research with children: background issues

This section outlines the reasons why it is beginning to be acknowledged that ignoring the child's voice in research which concerns him or her is morally wrong, goes against the way we now understand and conceptualise children and childhood, and produces inadequate research. It goes on to discuss why, traditionally, children have not been directly involved in research, and how that is beginning to change, but much less so for disabled children.

The child's right to be heard

Article 12 of the United Nations Convention on the Rights of the Child states that children have the right to say what they think about anything which affects them, and that what they say must be listened to carefully. From a total of 54 Articles, this is one of three *fundamental* rights of the child identified by the Convention. The UK Government agreed in 1992 to be bound by the Convention. So far, however, Article 12 has been found to be particularly *un*-implemented (Committee on the Rights of the Child, 1995), despite a number of recent developments in public policy which endorse its stance. The *Gillick* ruling in 1984, for example, advocated the consultation of children about decisions which affect their lives. The 1989 Children Act and the 1995 Children (Scotland) Act stress the importance of seeking the child's views on matters relating to his or her welfare, and involving him or her in decisions about the provision of welfare services. The Children's Services Plans which Social Services Departments are now legally obliged to produce likewise call for close consultation with children and attention to their views when designing services. The new NHS Patient's Charter for services for children and young people recognises children's rights to knowledge about their health care, and their legitimate expectations to be consulted, treated with respect and allowed as far as possible to be involved in choices about their care and treatment.

Changing perceptions of children – implications for research

The clear articulation in Article 12 of children's rights to express their views, and thereby promote their capacity to participate in and influence decisions about their lives, signals a change in the way children are perceived. Instead of being viewed as passive recipients of events impinging on their lives, they are recast as actively seeking to respond to, and shape, their social worlds. This reconceptualisation both mirrors and feeds into changes in the way children, and childhood, are conceived by various academic disciplines (Prout and James, 1990; Brannen and O'Brien, 1995). It also reflects new paradigms on how individuals (children and adults alike) manage their personal 'welfare', in which they are portrayed as actively managing their situations, as opposed to submitting passively to the events and situations they encounter (Titterton, 1992).

Viewing children as active social agents adds a further dimension to the *moral* case for involving them directly in research, as is implicit in Article 12. Theirs is clearly a perspective which cannot be second-guessed by adults speaking on their behalf – the approach which characterises most research on childhood so far.

Adults as proxies

The ability of adults to know what children think, feel or need, and thus act as their proxies in research has been challenged recently (Woodhead, 1990). Research which has consulted both adults and children has found consistent differences in the two groups' accounts.

For example, parents and children disagree about the nature of worries and concerns that siblings of a child with cancer may have (Menke, 1987), and the types of stresses associated with having a physical impairment (Tackett *et al.*, 1990). Parents have been shown to be more negative or pessimistic than their children when reporting their child's adjustment to chronic illness (Billings *et al.*, 1987; Ennett *et al.*, 1991), the self-image of adolescents with learning disabilities (Raviv and Stone, 1991), and children with cranio-facial deformities (LeFebvre and Munro, 1978).

What these, and other research findings, demonstrate is not necessarily that adults are 'wrong', rather that they experience the same event or situation differently, and are not capable of assuming the child's perspective. The accounts of two parents with disabled children acknowledge the gulf between their and their children's worlds. Featherstone (1980), writing about her son, stated:

It is almost impossible for us to imagine his world. (p.6)

Similarly, Greenfield (1970) notes:

> ... we are constantly trying to pierce his parameters. (p.69)

The issue is therefore one of children and adults existing in different cultures (Opie and Opie, 1991). The task of the researcher is to find ways of bridging that gap (Ritala-Koskinen, 1994). Working directly with children is essential to the success of that task. In other words *good* research on childhood needs to tap directly into the child's experience and views. Why, then, are children's views so consistently ignored in research on their lives?

Why children have not been directly involved in research

There are two main arguments against involving children directly in research (Mahon *et al.*, 1995). The first lies in the belief that children cannot be sources of 'valid data' (Qvortrup, 1994b). Secondly, there are significant ethical concerns about the vulnerability of children to exploitation or damage by researchers.

Data from children is unreliable and invalid

Children have been accused of not being mature enough to make judgements or to develop opinions, of not being capable of expressing themselves, and of being suggestible and unreliable (e.g. Ennett *et al.*, 1991). However, the foundation of these beliefs appears highly questionable.

> Some studies find that children are much more sophisticated than we have given them credit for. They are more verbally effective, emotionally considerate, or socially knowledgeable... We know

of no study that has found that children are more
'childish' than we have given them credit for.
(Fine and Sandstrom, 1988, p.72).

Research by Fivush *et al.* (1987), for example, found that
children as young as two years old could accurately
recall events that had occurred more than three months
previously. Two findings from Fivush's work have
wider implications for research with children. First,
where the child's accuracy of recall was questioned, it
tended to reflect problems in understanding what the
child was talking about, rather than the child reporting
inaccurate information. Secondly, the children recalled
particulars that the parents did not initially remember,
suggesting that children and adults place importance on
different aspects of an event.

Adolescents appear to be very aware of adults'
reluctance to place any credence on their views and
opinions.

> We were frequently struck by the extent to which
> our adolescent respondents felt short changed by
> the adults, including parents and teachers, with
> whom they came into contact. This was no mere
> teenage revolt against adults and adult authority.
> Rather, these young people were asking of adults
> that there should be greater reciprocity in their
> exchanges with them. The young people displayed
> complex and sophisticated awareness of the
> psychological and motivational processes under-
> lying adult identity, knowledge and authority. What
> they seemed to be asking for was a reflection of that
> maturity in adult representations of adolescents.
> (McGurk and Glachan, 1988, pp.33-34)

Indeed, it seems that any argument against the reliability or validity of children's accounts is equally applicable to adults' accounts (Williamson and Butler, 1994). Adults, as well as children, tell different stories on different occasions to different people. Research with adults often includes the problem of interpreting data collected from a social group different to that of the researchers (Alderson and Mayall, 1994; Ritala-Koskinen, 1994). And while we accuse children of being egocentric, are we not constrained by the 'adultcentric' nature of the way we perceive and understand the world (Goode, 1986)? Problems with researching children, therefore, appear to rest with the way the research is carried out and the data interpreted, rather than the fact that children are incapable of being 'good' research subjects (Fine and Sandstrom, 1988; Backett and Alexander, 1991).

Ethical objections

Concerns about the ethics of carrying out research directly with children has been a common reason in the past to use adults as proxy informants. Researchers today do not deny the particular vulnerability of children to abuse and exploitation in research. However, the approach taken now is to address the ethical issues that research with children raise, rather than use them as an excuse for shying away from talking directly to the child.

An increased awareness of the so-called 'social relations of research' enables researchers to work with children in ways that empower and benefit the child (Alderson, 1995). The social status of children – in particular, inequalities in status and power between children and adults – raises significant ethical issues with regard to research with children. It has been argued that these inequalities both make it hard for children to refuse to consent to take part in research, and that they have less power to influence the research process (Thompson, 1992; Alderson and Mayall, 1994). These issues are, perhaps, made more acute by the fact that, since much of applied social science research is about social problems, research involving children is often about sensitive or high risk events (Stanley and Sieber, 1992). It is also the case that it is the more vulnerable children, including those with impairments and disabilities, who are likely to be involved in research (Thompson, 1990).

All these issues are compounded by the fact that it is much harder to assess the risks associated with participating in social research compared to biomedical research (Koocher and Keith-Spiegal, 1994). Within social research, the risks to the child are often psychological, and may include fear of failure, threats to self-esteem, reactions to invasion of privacy, conflict or guilt and embarrassment. Such risks can be difficult to define, predict or assess, and the impact of research participation may be long term. It is also the case that the types of risk will vary according to the age of the child (Thompson, 1992). Young children have least social power, and will feel enormously constrained by the wishes of the adults around them. Older children taking part in research are more vulnerable to threats to their self-concept, and issues about privacy and conflict will increase.

Part of the problem of defining the risks of involvement in research comes from our lack of knowledge – from both adults and children – about what it is like to be a research subject. Experience from some fields of research suggests that certain concerns about the risks of taking part in research may be unfounded. Talking to dying children about their beliefs about death is a clear example of a research topic which would appear to be ethically questionable. Yet researchers have found that children do not find involvement with such research distressing. Rather it can offer children the chance to talk about their concerns and improve their understanding of what is happening to them (Spinetta and Deasy-Spinetta, 1981; Clunies-Ross and Lansdown, 1988). However, it is important to stress here that these research projects were handled with extreme sensitivity, and the positive outcome of being involved in these studies was dependent on the careful approach taken.

A later section of our report will discuss strategies which can be applied throughout the research process to address the ethical demands of research with children. For further discussion of this issue, we would refer the reader to Alderson's (1995) excellent discussion paper.

Finally, an equally pressing ethical issue must be that children's opinions have been consistently ignored by researchers and practitioners, and that services and interventions for children have been instigated without consulting the children themselves. An example here concerns children's experience of pain. Despite considerable research interest into pain, children and young people's experience of pain has been ignored in the past (Ross and Ross, 1984). Assumptions were made that infants do not experience pain and that young children are less sensitive to pain than adults. Strategies for pain management in children and young people have therefore been developed on the basis of virtual ignorance of what pain feels like to a child. The goal of research must now be to give children a voice through ethically and methodologically sound work.

Recent developments

In recent years researchers from a wide variety of disciplines have acknowledged their failure to consult directly with children (e.g. Ambert, 1986; Prout and James, 1990; Kalnins *et al.*, 1992; Qvortup, 1994a). The cultural presumption that what children might have to say is of little interest or importance has been challenged (Williamson and Butler, 1994). The so-called 'boom' in research on childhood within the field of sociology is reflected in a burgeoning of child-centred research in other social sciences, notably education, psychology, health promotion and social policy. A series of major research programmes funded by the Economic and Social Research Council (Children 5 – 16), the Department of Health (Parenting; Mother and Child Health) and the Joseph Rowntree Foundation has emphasised the importance of eliciting children's views, and contributed to the growing consensus that this research is both important and practicable. It is possible, then, to see signs of increasing participation by children in research which concerns their lives.

This is much less true of disabled children, who remain a highly neglected group (Cheston, 1994). Yet the reasons for directly seeking these children's accounts of their lives, their preferences for how professionals of various kinds should relate to them, and the kinds of support services they would find most helpful, are compelling. We need to know about these things at first hand to make progress in helping children to achieve the best possible quality of life, to maximise the control they can exercise in their lives, and to prevent abuse. Moreover, the policy developments noted above – new children's legislation, the drawing up of children's services plans, and the new NHS charter for children's services – clearly require research which engages directly with children who are disabled or ill so that services, and professionals, respond more sensitively to their needs.

The next Chapter reviews what the available literature has to say about how children, and particularly disabled children, can be involved in research and the appropriateness, and merits, of different approaches to accessing their views.

The research approach

Having established that children should and must be involved in research, the first key question which needs to be addressed concerns the best way of accessing their views. Essentially the choice lies between adopting a quantitative or qualitative approach.

Qualitative techniques provide those involved with research with a more direct voice than is possible through participation in quantitative research, for example experiments or surveys (Prout and James, 1990). Qualitative research refers to a number of research approaches which seek to describe, interpret and understand phenomena. It has been described as empathetic since its goal is 'to approximate the perspectives of others' (Ferguson et al., 1992a, p.6). In other words, central importance is given to individual accounts, and frequently voiced themes as well as more divergent perspectives are both used by the researcher in seeking to answer the research questions. Quantitative research, in contrast, aims to define and predict phenomena using a number of pre-defined factors, and the significance, or explanatory power, of out-liers is underplayed (Krahn et al., 1995).

Qualitative research uses three main methodological techniques – interviews, observation and the analysis of formal and informal documents, such as photographs, diaries and official policy statements.

Using qualitative techniques for disability research

Over recent years there has been an increase in the use of qualitative research techniques within the fields of disability research. A key factor in the emergence of this research approach has been the growing recognition of the need to discover the views and experiences of disabled people themselves, rather than to rely on information collected from proxies such as parents, teachers and other practitioners (e.g. Bogdan and Taylor, 1976). In addition, specialist academic and professional journals, which ten years ago would have been predominated by quantitative studies, now condone and encourage the use of qualitative research techniques (Ferguson *et al.*, 1992a).

It has long been acknowledged that qualitative methods are particularly suited to giving voice to the 'underdog' in society (Becker, 1966/7) – people who are often the subject of research, yet whose voices are rarely heard. Becker argued that qualitative research challenges the 'hierarchy of credibility' which gives more credence to the opinions and experiences of those with greater social power. As well as its underlying philosophy, it is the techniques typical of qualitative research – interviews, observation, written material – which enable access to groups of people who would be simply 'unavailable' if quantitative techniques were used (Ferguson *et al.*, 1992b). Disabled people are a particularly pertinent example of these people whose voices were never heard. As Gerber (1990) states:

> ...people with disabilities were little more than objects of study. Their voice had less legitimacy and less authority than that of the medical,

rehabilitation, educational and welfare bureaucracy professionals who studied and worked with them. Generally these experts have been well-meaning people, who have urged compassion and responsibility on societies guilty of cruelty or indifference. But their conceptions of disability and of disabled people gave rise to the development of social policy that imposed, in the name of benign paternalism, bureaucratic manipulation and socio-economic dependence, and ultimately dead-end lives, on people with disabilities.
(p.4)

Research approaches and models of disability

The different philosophies underlying qualitative and quantitative research are also reflected in the way disability is conceptualised and the types of research question it engenders. There are two main models of disability: the medical model and the social model.

Quantitative research on disability tends to align itself with the medical model of disability. Disability is seen as a 'problem' located entirely within the individual. The research emphasis has therefore been on measurement, of the severity of the 'problem' and its prevalence (e.g. Martin et al., 1988; Bone and Meltzer, 1989). The focus of research is narrow, concentrating only on the impairment or condition, rather than on the effects of the interaction between society, the environment and the impairment on an individual's life.

In contrast, the social model of disability argues that disability is socially produced (Oliver, 1990). The 'problem' therefore lies with society and structural factors which fail to take account or adapt to people with physical or learning impairments. Qualitative research seeks to base itself on this model of disability:

> Interpretivitism *or the qualitative approach* maintains that disability is not a fact or an entity, whose nature is just waiting to be discovered. Disability is rather an experience waiting to be described, or, more precisely, a social construction of multiple experiences waiting to be recognised.
> (Ferguson *et al.*, 1992b, p.296)

However, disabled people have argued that while an interpretivist or qualitative approach may be the right way to go as far as research *methodology* is concerned, significant change is still needed in terms of the whole *research process*.

> ...Interpretive research still has a relatively small group of powerful experts doing work on a larger number of relatively powerless research subjects.
> (Oliver, 1992, p.106)

Thus Oliver argues that interpretive or qualitative research will be no more 'emancipatory' for disabled people than objective or quantitative research until the 'social relations of research production' also change (p.106). This will require greater dialogue between researcher and disabled people throughout the entire research process, beginning with the identification of key issues, through the development of a research question, formulating the research design, collecting and interpreting the data, to, finally, the ownership and dissemination of the research findings (Oliver, 1992; Barnes, 1992). Such an approach to research would, it is argued, 'go some way to shift the balance of power between the researcher and the researched' (Barnes, 1992, p.123). We return to these issues in a later section when we consider how disabled children can be greater empowered in the process of research.

Using quantitative and qualitative research techniques together

There will be occasions, however, when the research question demands the use of scales, measures or other questionnaires. In these instances, preliminary work using qualitative techniques will ensure that the research tools constructed are relevant and appropriate. Individual interviews (e.g. Claflin and Barbarin, 1991; Berry *et al.*, 1993; Havermans and Eiser, 1994; Eiser *et al.*, 1995) and group discussions (e.g. Mates and Allison, 1992; Telfair *et al.*, 1994; Hoppe *et al.*, 1995) have both been used to develop measures subsequently used on a larger sample. Such measures are far more likely to appeal and be salient to other child respondents, as well as having face validity. In addition, if the respondents know that the measure was developed in consultation with children, it may make it easier for them to admit to negative feelings or experiences, in the knowledge that these have been raised by others and therefore validate their own experiences.

Doing research with children: why and how it needs to be different

The fact that we have all been children, that children live within adult society, and that children look like adults can lull researchers into assuming that research with children demands no changes in the way we do research (Fine and Sandstrom, 1988).

However, a review of the literature clearly shows that researchers do need to recognise that the differences between adult and child extend far beyond developmental differences, or levels of maturity. It is not a question of coming down to their level, rather it is recognising that, in some ways, the process of research with children needs to be different to that with adults (Ritala-Koskinen, 1994). This will include the methodologies used, especially when working with young children (Oakley *et al.*, 1995), and the way we talk to children.

> ...as...researchers we find ourselves in interaction with children to whom we are unfamiliar. What children make of these situations will very much influence their response to them. For example, what an unfamiliar adult means by a question may turn out to be quite different from what the child thinks the question means.
> (McGurk and Glachan, 1988, p.21)

It also requires that account is taken of the fact that children and adults exist within different cultures (Tammivaara and Enright, 1986), which has significant implications for the way data is analysed and interpreted.

> What we attempt to discover about children is dependent on our learning how they comprehend and construct the world...and this is itself dependent on the necessity of crossing over to share their view of the world.
> (Silvers, 1976, p.49)

Children's views of the world are different

Differences in cognitive development and life experiences, and the fact that children exist in a different culture to adults, all contribute to the fact that a child's view of events and situations will differ from that of adults.

Children actively try to make sense of situations and events they encounter and their 'construction of reality' may differ from that of adults (Bronfenbrenner, 1979; Mackay, 1991). A child's knowledge is based on the experiences they have. Thus, for example, a young child whose only experience of hospitals has been the admission and subsequent death of a grandparent will believe that people go to hospital to die, rather than to get better (Eiser, 1990). In addition, the way a child makes sense of events will depend on their cognitive development or maturity. An example here comes from research with chronically ill children (Brewster, 1982). While five year old children believed that doctors deliberately mean to hurt them, seven year old children accepted that doctors did not mean to hurt them, but believed they did not care about the pain they inflicted. Beliefs were different among 11 year old children who thought that doctors realised they were inflicting pain, but did not understand how much it hurt.

Other research has shown that children and adults find different events, or aspects of events, important or salient. One example given by Fivush *et al.* (1987) concerns mothers and young children's recall of the birth of a sibling. While this is a highly significant event for the mother, none of the children in Fivush's study could recall anything substantial about the birth of their brother or sister. Other research suggests that very young children simply do not find this event interesting enough to remember in the first place (Sheingold and Tenney, 1982). In the past, researchers may have interpreted such findings as an indicator of poor memory in children. Instead, it appears to be a case of researchers taking an adult perspective to the worlds of children, and making assumptions about what is important to a child. This has significant implications both for the sorts of issues that should be the object of research, as well as the assumptions made about the topics covered by, say, a research interview (Tammivaara and Enright, 1986). A approach which takes the lead from the child would seem to be the best response to this particular problem.

In this orientation, interviews can be understood as a joint product of what interviewees and interviewers talk about together and how they talk with each other. This puts brakes on the understanding of the interviewer as having total power in interview situations. Instead the

interviewee is understood as actively constructing meaning on the base of his/her own life.
(Ritala-Koskinen, 1994, p.313)

Bearison (1991) described this process as remaining within the 'psychological space' of the child. In doing so, he argued, it is possible to use questions and comments to encourage children to elaborate on issues and events that *they* deem relevant.

Accounting for cognitive development

In this and the following section we consider the impact of the development of a child's cognitive and communicative abilities on the research process. It is important to point out at the outset of this discussion that children are a highly heterogeneous group and issues related to differences in development or maturity apply equally to research with children of different ages as to research with children and adults.

It is from the field of child abuse that the impact of developmental factors on the interviewing process have been most closely explored. The findings of research of this kind are contained in an excellent review by Steward *et al.* (1993). Key points arising from their review are summarised in this and the following section.

First, there is considerable variation in ability among children of the same age. This represents a change in thinking from the strictly Piagetian view of cognitive development which believed that children's thinking evolves through a fixed sequence of stages.

Secondly, even very young children can recall routine and novel events and can be logical about events that have meaning for their lives. Likewise, recall of complex events significantly improves if the event is broken down into a number of simpler units. It is, perhaps, differences in the way children's cognitive development has been tested or assessed that have led to these neo-Piagetian theories being developed. In particular, it has been found that children's performance is enhanced when tasks relate to meaningful, real-life experiences. (Piagetian research typically used non-meaningful events or situations.) Similarly, other researchers have found that children under the age of around eight years find it difficult to talk about abstract concepts, for example, health (Backett and Alexander, 1991).

Thirdly, children, especially young children, rely on context and cues in recalling and describing events or situations.

> Questions may serve as a type of external cue, as may certain props or re-exposure to a room or location where an event has occurred. A young child who can recall little about what happened may be able to answer many (but not all) simple questions accurately or act out the event with a single toy (or set of simple toys) or anatomical dolls. (Steward *et al.*, 1993, p.26)

Fourthly, like adults, children do not tend to recall events inaccurately or introduce fantasy into their reports. Where the child appears to be making errors or being fanciful this may actually be due problems of communication between the child and adult. Steward *et al.* (1993) give the following example:

A young child might report that 'the dog flew through the air' without telling the interviewer it was a puppet that the child pretended could fly. Differentiating such errors of communication from errors of confabulation can be a difficult task. (p.27)

Finally, for 'optimal performance', children need an emotionally supportive environment. Intimidation may not only cause a child to stop responding to questions, it may also increase young children's suggestibility.

Development of communicative competence

Understanding of a child's capacity to communicate is vital if researchers are to obtain valid and reliable information.

It does little good to ask children long complex questions containing embedded clauses or double negatives when they can understand sentences only six to eight words long. Young children may respond only to that part of the question that they understand, ignoring other parts that might be crucial to the adult's concern. The result can be a sense of contradiction and inconsistency for the adult.
(Steward *et al.*, 1993, p.27)

Overall, Steward *et al.* (1993) recommend, on the basis of the literature they reviewed, the use of short sentences, short questions and simple language when interviewing children, especially younger children. In other words, it is important that the interviewer adopts the child's level of communicative ability.

Figure 1 below provides a summary of the stages of language development.

Figure 1: Stages of language development

Age	Level of communicative ability
10–13 months	First words. Single utterances but understand much more.
18–22 months	Vocabulary of around 50 words. Can put two or more words together into phrases.
2 years	Using 2–3 word utterances, but language telegraphic. Use content words (nouns, verbs) and omit function words (pronouns, articles and prepositions).
Pre-schoolers	Have adequate vocabulary to talk about the 'here and now'. Can describe past events but their use of past tense and their conceptions of time not well developed.
5–6 years	Can consistently answer 'why', 'when', or 'how' questions.
5–10 years	Gradual increase in understanding and use of more complex language.

Interpretation and analysis of verbal and written material

The discussion so far has focused on the way the differences between adults and children need to be accounted for in a research interview. Equally important, however, is that this understanding of differences in 'culture', cognitive development and communicative competence are carried through to the stage of data analysis and interpretation. One way of overcoming the possibility of mis-interpretation of information is to give feedback to and consult with the children after the data analysis stage in order to check the researchers' interpretation of the children's accounts.

The nature of the research encounter

We have already explored the numerous ways in which children differ from adults. These differences have significant implications for quite practical aspects of the way we carry out research with children. For instance, research suggests that children, especially very young children, are more sensitive than adults to aspects of the researchers' appearance or personality (Koocher and Keith-Spiegel, 1994).

Context

It is also important to consider the context and environment in which the research encounter takes place. For children of any age, the context can significantly affect a child's ability to communicate (Reich, 1986). A context which we, as adults, find familiar, and therefore are aware of the role we are expected to assume, can be quite alien to a child. Very young children do not, for instance, generally sit and have face-to-face conversations with adults, especially a strange adult. Most conversations occur alongside other activities and usually relate to those activities. Thus what would be a typical setting for a research interview with an adult is inappropriate for children, especially younger age groups.

Young children generally find *doing* something *with* something and talking about that something to be easier, more comfortable, and more interesting than only talking about something that isn't physically present.
(Tammivaara and Enright, 1986, p.232)

Bearison's (1991) work with children with cancer demonstrates the importance of working alongside children as opposed to being formal and directive. Bearison believes that the reason he obtained such frank and open accounts from the children he studied was because he went, on a number of occasions, *to* the children and joined in *their* activities. It was during the course of these interactions that he was able to explore with the children their experiences of having cancer. Fivush *et al.* (1987) used a similar approach to explore two year old children's recall of past events. The researchers refer to their interactions with the children as conversations that occurred as they played with the child at their own home. It is interesting to note that while the researcher spent between one to two hours with the child, the actual time spent talking about past events (the research topic) was only about 30 minutes. Ross and Ross (1984) reiterate this point, stating that the interview should feel like a conversation rather than a test.

To this end the interviewer should appear cheerful, relaxed and unhurried. There must be no feeling of disapproval conveyed for slow or minimal responses.
(p.76)

Building rapport
This brings us on to the more general issue of the importance of building up rapport between the

researcher and the child. Researchers who have worked with children frequently report that for a research interview to be successful, for both child and researcher, it is important to invest time at the beginning of a session building up a friendly and informal relationship with the child (Tammivaara and Enright, 1986: Bearison, 1991). It might be appropriate to visit the child on more than one occasion in order to develop a relationship in which the child feels comfortable enough to respond to the researcher's questions (Lentz, 1985). This may be particularly true for children with learning difficulties. Booth and Booth's (1994) research with adults with learning difficulties involved a number of interviews with each individual. They found that, for some informants, it was only after a number of interviews that sufficient rapport and trust had developed for the individuals to reveal certain information.

> Rather than being an indulgence, trust and rapport may have a crucial influence on the quality of data obtained.
> (Booth and Booth, 1994, p.418)

Ross and Ross (1984) stress the importance of the warm-up questions in setting the whole tenor of the interview. Such questions should be easy to answer, thus instilling confidence in the child that he or she will be able contribute successfully in the interview.

> ...the child is the expert and his status as such should be made clear to him. It is equally important to make the child feel confident at the outset of his capability of functioning effectively in the interview situation. A stumbling, awkward start may jeopardize the rest of the interview. A powerful

procedure for instilling confidence is the warm-up
question cluster followed immediately by a replay
of the tape. The warm-up question cluster is a
group of simple factual questions that the child is
virtually certain to be able to answer unhesitatingly.
(p.76)

Using more than one interview session

Other reasons for repeated visits may be not wanting to
tire the child, or difficulties retaining the child's
attention (Ritchie *et al.*, 1984). This may be especially so
for very young children, children who are sick and
those with learning difficulties. The duration of any
session should be led by the child. It is interesting to
note, however, that researcher and practitioners may
underestimate how long children want to 'talk' about
something that is important to them (Marchant and
Page, 1993).

Using a familiar interviewer

A number of papers suggest that researchers may not
always be the best people to carry out interviews with
children since they are unfamiliar figures (e.g. Koocher,
1981; Lentz, 1985). Brofenbrenner (1979) argued that in
order to achieve ecological validity in research,
especially where a child is being asked to do unfamiliar
tasks in unfamiliar settings, it is necessary to involve
familiar people in the process of investigation. Certainly
strange people and strange situations do seem to
influence the rate and quality of responses by children
(e.g. Lentz, 1985). However, in some cases the topic of
the research may make it wholly inappropriate to use a
parent or teacher as the interviewer. Problems of
ensuring that familiar adults are sufficiently skilled to

carry out the interviews would need to be addressed. Another solution to this problem, and one which we have already mentioned, would be for the researcher to spend more time developing relationships and building up rapport with the children involved in the research.

Addressing the ethical issues of researching children

A number of professional bodies offer guidelines about the ethics of research and these are equally applicable and an important resource to researchers who work with children (British Psychological Society, 1991; Medical Research Council, 1991; British Paediatric Association, 1992; British Sociological Association, 1993). We have already described how children are particularly vulnerable to exploitation or abuse by researchers, and that factors contributing to this vulnerability differ according to the child's age. In this section, therefore, we consider the practical aspects of ensuring that a research project with children adequately addresses these particular ethical demands. There are two key issues: informed consent and dealing with disclosure.

Optimising informed consent

In legal terms, 16 years is taken as the age at which it is not necessary to obtain the parent's consent as well as the child's for medical or dental treatment (the Family Law Reform Act, 1968). However, the Act does not stipulate the age at which children can give effective consent, and the emphasis rests on judgements about an individual child's competence.

> Children who are judged to be competent have certain consent rights. Legal views of children's competence to consent give less emphasis to a

stated age of consent, and more emphasis on individual ability or competence, as shown by the Gillick case.

(Alderson, 1995, p.71)

In the *Gillick* case (1985) the Law Lords defined a competent child to be one who 'achieves a sufficient understanding and intelligence to enable him or her to understand fully what is proposed', and also has 'sufficient discretion to enable him or her to make a wise choice in his or her own interests'.

Just as researchers now acknowledge that adult proxies do not provide the same information as the children themselves, it is no longer acceptable to obtain consent to take part in research from a parent or teacher on behalf of the child. Indeed, the age at which researchers should independently seek the child's consent is much lower than that laid down in legislation. Thus the issue of understanding and competence to give consent become even more potent issues, especially when the research concerns very young children or those with learning difficulties.

Informed consent has three characteristics (Bersoff and Hofer, 1990): (i) it is based on knowledge – gained by means of information presented in understandable terms; (ii) it is voluntary; and (iii) the individual has the capacity or competence to give consent. Each of these aspects of informed consent presents particular problems for research with children on a number of counts (Thompson, 1990; Powell and Vacha-Haase, 1994).

First, limited cognitive understanding and lack of previous experience of research participation make it difficult for a child to understand what it means to be involved with research (Forman and Ladd, 1991; Thompson, 1992). This means that special care needs to be taken to provide age-appropriate information which should be provided verbally and in an attractive written and/or pictorial form, or, if more appropriate, a tape recording or video (Tymchuk, 1994). Secondly, children have been socialised to do what adults tell them, and they know that the consequences of not doing what they are told are often unpleasant (Keith-Spiegal, 1983). It is vital that the child understands that participation in a research project is voluntary, confidential and can stop at any time (Ross and Ross, 1984). The child must also be aware that there is nothing wrong with refusing to take part, and this right to refuse must be respected by researchers and parents (Powell and Vacha-Haase, 1994).

Dealing with disclosure

In the course of carrying out research with children, there is the possibility that a child might disclose some information which suggests that he or she is significantly 'at risk' in some way. It might be that the child is being abused, or that the child is indulging in certain behaviours (e.g. drug taking) that threaten their welfare, or that the child is, for one reason or another, highly disturbed or distressed. It may be that the topic of a research project will mean that such cases are likely to come to light, and then it is likely that the researcher will be more prepared to deal with them. However, all researchers working with children should consider how they might deal with a disclosure which they find disturbing and feel should be referred to an expert of some sort.

Where the researcher anticipates disclosures, the most appropriate course of action may be to state in the consent information that certain behaviours will be discussed with, or referred to, a responsible adult so that the child can be helped (Rotheram-Borus and Koopman, 1994). Researchers should consider whether, as part of their project, they need to set up or co-ordinate some form of follow-up support service to deal with disclosures or requests for help. Whether or not parents are also informed of the child's disclosure will depend on the child's age. For children under 16 years of age, one would expect to inform the parents too, but the child should be told that this will happen. Whatever the age, the child should be kept fully informed both about the researcher's concern and their intended actions (Kinard, 1985).

Children with learning difficulties

The ethical principles which apply to children with learning difficulties are the same as for all children, though it is clear that they are a particularly vulnerable group, especially in terms of a lowered sense of autonomy and the ability to understand the consequences of consenting to take part in a piece of research (Biklen and Moseley, 1988). Booth and Booth (1994) have extensive experience of carrying out research with adults with learning difficulties, and many of the procedures they adopt in their research also apply to children with learning difficulties.

With respect to obtaining consent, Booth and Booth adopted a cautious and unrushed approach. The research was introduced to the individuals by a professional worker whom the person with learning difficulties knew and liked. The workers decided when and how to introduce the possibility of taking part in the research and individuals' names were only passed to the researcher if they agreed to see the researcher. There are advantages and disadvantages to this approach but it certainly overcame the problem of confidentiality and made refusal easier. Booth and Booth also believe that it made the first interview less stressful because the individuals had agreed to see them and had some idea of what the research was about. The disadvantages include the fact that the researchers could not control the way the research was presented, and that the relationship between the worker and the potential recruit might affect how they responded to the invitation to take part in the research.

During the first visit to a person's home, the researchers devoted considerable time to simply providing information about themselves, the study and what taking part in the research would involve. It was then up to the individuals whether or not another meeting was arranged, and where it should take place.

Finally, the researchers found that it was often necessary to remind their informants that they were researchers rather than welfare workers. While this might not be a particular issue for children with learning difficulties, it is probably the case that these children will need to be given information on more than one occasion about the research, confidentiality, and being able to withdraw involvement at any time.

Research techniques

This section looks more closely at one part of the research process - data collection. The three kinds of research technique most commonly used in qualitative research are individual interviews, group discussions and observation. Each will be discussed in terms of adapting their use to research with children. The final part of this section considers specific research tools which tend to be used alongside interviews, including the use of drawing and written material, visual analogues, play interviews and semi-projective techniques.

Individual interviews

Interviews are a means of data collection used by both quantitative and qualitative researchers. For the quantitative researcher, however, the interview can be conceived as a verbally administered questionnaire consisting of 'closed' or fixed response questions. The format of the interview is highly structured, having been developed and constructed prior to fieldwork. Qualitative interviewing, in contrast, is governed to some extent by the interviewee. The interview might include some structured questions but it will also always include a more unstructured session. Within the unstructured, or in-depth, part of the interview the researcher will have a set of topics to be covered but the questioning evolves as a result of the interaction between interviewer and interviewee. Thus quantitative interviews *supply* information whereas as qualitative interviews *generate* information (Ross and Ross, 1984).

The type of research approach taken will obviously depend on the research question. Factual information can be collected using structured interviews. But where the research seeks to find out about experiences, opinions, reasons and ideas, unstructured interviews are essential. This section discusses the importance of language, the way questions are asked, and how drawing, writing and pictures can be used to facilitate the in-depth interview.

Adopting the child's language

The need for the researcher to adopt the child's level of communicative ability has already been discussed. In addition, it is essential that the interviewer employs the words and phrases the child uses in relation to the research topic. Children and families often develop their own vocabulary for a specific issue. For example, in her interviews with children with epilepsy, Beresford (1992) found that some children did not use the words fit or seizure. Instead words such as 'funnies', 'turns', 'blanks' and 'falls' were used. The phrases and words used by the child need to be established at the beginning of the interview. In some cases, it may help to ask the parent beforehand about the way something is referred to by the family.

The spaced question approach

Ross and Ross (1984) recommend spacing questions about a particular topic throughout the interview. This allows exploration of the topic within a number of discussions about different issues, all of which relate to the research topic. The researchers state: 'By spacing the assessment of the topic, opportunities are provided for the retrieval of information that had not occurred to the child on the initial presentation of the topic' (p.75).

Thus in their research on children's experience of pain, they asked essentially the same question at three different stages of the interview. First, during discussions about the family, the children were asked to say how they would describe a migraine headache to their mother; later, in the context of a conversation about school and friends, to say how they would describe the pain to their best friend; finally, when talking about doctors, to say what they would tell a doctor about having a migraine. The authors found that, although there was some overlap, different sorts of information were revealed in response to the three questions. Typically, the descriptions they gave to their mothers were concise and unemotional, whereas to the best friend the child provided a highly emotive account in which the discomfort was emphasised. The most complete account was obtained in response to the request to imagine they were describing the pain to a doctor. Unfortunately, the authors do not discuss whether they believe that this full account to doctors was because it followed previous questions about describing pain, or whether the children perceived differences in what their mothers, best friends and doctors should know.

Drawing and writing as facilitators in a research interview

Drawings, as well as play, are often viewed as belonging to the child's, as opposed to the adult's world (Levin,

1994) and offer a 'window in children's perceptions of the social world' (Rubenstein *et al.*, 1987, p.245). As a result, they are used in a number of ways in research with children. First, they can be used to assess the child's development (e.g. Goodenough, 1926) or their psychological well-being (e.g. DiLeo, 1970). Secondly, they can be an actual source of data – we discuss this in two later sections. Finally, and often as a 'by-product' of using them for one of the other two purposes, drawing and writing can be used as a means of opening communication between an adult and a child. Thus Levin (1994) used drawings as a source of data as well as a means of facilitating her interviews with children about their perceptions of family and step-family members. In Backett and Alexander's (1991) work on young children's beliefs about health, the children were sent a drawing pad prior to the research visit and asked to draw foods and activities that were healthy and unhealthy. As well as using these drawings as a source of data, the authors noted that:

> Asking the children to talk about their drawings was a good way to begin the interview. It created a rapport and gave the children a basic framework to explain about keeping healthy.
> (p.36)

Pictures and photographs as facilitators

Pictures or photographs are often used in research with children as a means of providing visual cues of the topics being covered in an interview (e.g. Curry and Russ, 1985; Eiser *et al.*, 1990; Backett and Alexander, 1991). Photographs can be particularly useful since they can be personalised. A researcher who used pictures when talking to children about their experiences and likes and dislikes of respite care believes that photographs of the actual facilities used by a child would have proved even more productive (Robinson, 1995).

Pictures or photographs can also be used as materials for a task or game which forms part of the research interview. In Backett and Alexander's (1991) work on children's concepts of healthy foods and activities, children were asked to post pictures of healthy and unhealthy foods and activities into one of two post boxes. They were also asked to rank a series of seven pictures of activities from the most healthy to the most unhealthy. The child was then asked to explain the order they had chosen.

If pictures are used, then there are a number of practical suggestions. First, they should be large, simple, realistic and of high quality (Stewig, 1994; Lauroul, 1995). The materials used should be durable so that the children can handle them freely: it may for instance be well worth having them laminated. There are a number of organisations which produce resource packs of drawings relevant to children and disability which are copyright free. Alternatively an illustrator can be employed to produce pictures for a particular project.

Finally, the use of pictures in interviews should be carefully piloted. It is important that children perceive the pictures in the way intended. In addition, researchers should be prepared to discontinue using visual cues where they appear to be more of a distraction than an aid (Fivush *et al.*, 1987).

Using audio-visual cues

A relatively recent development has been the use of tape-recordings or video vignettes to facilitate interviews. Beresford (1992) used video vignettes of a series of stressful situations in order to explore the coping strategies used by healthy children and children with epilepsy to deal with these situations. The technique worked well, serving to maintain the child's interest and aid recall. In addition, for some children, being able to identify themselves with the main character in the vignettes (a boy and girl version were produced) enabled them to talk more freely about their experiences of stressful or sensitive situations such as being teased.

Group discussions or focus groups

Focus groups are open-ended discussions, usually between seven and ten individuals, which are facilitated by a moderator. In the past, focus groups were the domain of market research; recently, however, they have been increasingly used by social scientists (Basch, 1987). Group discussions or focus groups are not the cheap option to individual interviews. They have a different research function and are only appropriate for particular research questions (Hoppe *et al.*, 1995). There are a number of differences between the data collected from an individual interview and a focus group (Basch, 1987; Folch-Lyon and Trost, 1981; MacDonald and Topper, 1989). Such data will first include the opinions and experiences of a group of people; secondly, provide information on the process of the development of ideas and the negotiations which occur between group members; and thirdly, if this is the purpose of the group, will generate a collective response to a research question or task.

Quite a number of projects have used focus groups in their research with children. The consensus is that, when used appropriately, it is a highly suitable research technique for use with children and young people (Alderson, 1995). The interactive and supportive nature of a focus group seems to encourage more reticent children to offer information that they might not provide in an individual interview (Mates and Allison, 1992; Hoppe *et al.*, 1995). Thus far focus groups have mainly been used to inform the process of questionnaire design or the development of measures (e.g. Roberts *et al.*, 1988; Telfair *et al.*, 1994; Mates and Allison, 1992; Hoppe *et al.*, 1995). In addition, Oakley *et al.* (1995) used them to round off sessions held with groups of school children who had, individually, produced drawings and written accounts of their beliefs about health and cancer.

Adapting the group discussion technique for research with children

As part of the development of a series of measures, Hoppe *et al.* (1995) used group discussions to explore children's understanding of health, sexuality and AIDS, as well as to find out about the sort of language children use in relation to these issues. The authors were positive about the value of focus groups and, based on their experiences, made the following recommendations about using focus groups with children. First, Hoppe *et al.* felt that the optimum size of group was five children - fewer than tends to be recommended for adult groups. Secondly, the children should be grouped according to age and, if necessary or appropriate given the research topic, there should be separate sex groups. Mates and Allison (1992) also noted a gender effect on children's participation in discussions, though this seemed to interact with academic ability too. Thirdly, researchers should not expect to cover more than one major topic per session. Finally, the length of the meeting should be limited, taking account of the children's ages.

Leading a focus group

It is important to remember that, as with in-depth individual interviews, the quality of data collected during a group discussion is dependent on the skills of the facilitator (Festervand, 1984-1985). Using professional, freelance facilitators may be the best option for unskilled researchers, though it will be necessary to provide training about the particular research area. For a detailed consideration of focus group methodology the reader is referred to Krueger (1988) and Morgan (1988).

Group discussions without a facilitator

Although there is very little published research, there is a growing interest among social scientists in holding group discussions without the presence of an adult or facilitator. Wade and Moore (1993) used this technique in their research into children's experiences of special education. Pupils were asked to discuss their experiences of school life and these conversations were recorded. This material was used in conjunction with data collected using other techniques including questionnaires and sentence completion tasks.

Observational techniques

There are a number of levels to approaching the collection of observational data which are dependent on the degree to which the researcher integrates or merges into the social context of the research topic. First is the *complete participant* approach where the researcher conceals his or her purpose and assumes a new identity in order to become a member of the social group under investigation. An excellent example of this approach is Goffman's (1961) study of the lives of people in hospital with a mental illness. Secondly, the researcher can be a *participant observer*. In this instance the researcher joins or attaches him or herself to representatives of the social group under investigation, but the group know the researcher's identity and the reason for his or her presence (Gold, 1994). Thirdly, is the *detached observer*. In this case the researcher does not directly interact with the individuals under observation.

A major criticism of observational techniques is that the presence of a researcher inevitably affects the interactions and behaviours of those under observation (e.g. Barnes, 1992). Becoming a 'familiar face' may address the problem to some extent, though this becomes more difficult when researching children, especially in settings where adults are not usually present. Although researchers have claimed to be able to achieve a so-called 'least-adult role' whilst observing children (Waksler, 1986; Mandell, 1988), others have argued that, just as with other qualitative research techniques, it is better to accept and work with the cultural and developmental differences between adults and children rather than assume they can be overcome (Fine and Sandstrom, 1988).

Virtually all the research using observational techniques with disabled children and young people has been concerned with describing and assessing behaviour problems, reactions to painful procedures (e.g. Katz *et al.*, 1980) and how children cope with medical stressors (e.g. Tarnow and Gutstein, 1983; Hubert *et al.*, 1988). All these studies used the detached observer approach. There are limitations to the data collected through detached observation alone (Le Baron and Zeltzer, 1984; Miller *et al.*, 1992). The researcher has no access to the cognitive processes and reasoning underlying the observed behaviours. Thus the possibility exists for both misinterpretation of the behavioural data, as well as the research failing to include and report information which cannot be collected using observational techniques. It is for these reasons that it is best to use observation with self-report techniques.

We could find no research with disabled children in which the more participative approaches were used, such as the complete participant or participant observer approach, to explore their experiences of disability. We have already pointed out the difficulties with adult researchers adopting the complete participant approach for research with children. However, research with disabled adults does suggest that observation techniques can be a powerful way of exploring the experiences of disabled people (e.g. Barnes, 1992; Gold, 1994).

Particular research tools
Drawings and written material as a source of data
Asking children to draw or write stories is becoming an increasingly common data collection technique used with younger children (e.g. Backett and Alexander, 1991; Levin, 1994). The more specialised approach of using drawings and written material as a semi-projective technique is discussed later.

Usually, the data collected from drawings or writing supplement an interview. However, Morrow (1992) only used the written accounts of children's out-of-school activities. She believed that children's written descriptions would provide more data in a shorter time than would be collected through a questionnaire. Certainly for older children, using the so-called essay method (Millde, 1991) can provide in-depth information. Brodin and Millde's work on the psychosocial aspects of brittle bone disease included a study in which adolescents wrote about their lives, their hopes for the future and how they viewed their condition (Millde, 1990; Brodin, 1993). Clearly this particular technique is only suitable for children who are competent and confident writers. If not, the child will find involvement in the study damaging to their self-esteem, and the researcher will obtain incomplete and inadequate material. A less demanding approach to collecting written material, and therefore useful for younger children and those with learning difficulties, is the use of sentence completion tasks. Typically, these tasks are used alongside a number of research tools (e.g. Wade and Moore, 1993). Sentence completion may also be a useful approach when the research concerns issues that are sensitive or potentially embarrassing (Cavet, 1996).

Using drawings with younger children can mean that they can be included in studies despite their limited verbal (and writing) skills. LeFebvre and Munro (1978) used younger children's drawings of themselves in their work on self-concepts of children with cranio-facial abnormalities before and after surgery; the older children completed a rating scale instead. There are some limitations to using drawings. Certain research topics do not lend themselves to this technique, especially if they concern rather abstract concepts. In addition, the child's drawing ability may result in certain items being drawn and others not (Backett and Alexander, 1991).

The 'write and draw' technique, as the name implies, uses both drawing and a written account. Among older children, this may overcome the problem of differences in drawing ability affecting the data collected. 'Write and draw' was used successfully by Oakley *et al.* (1995) in their study of children's beliefs about health and cancer. The drawings were scanned and stored onto a computer from which they were retrieved for analysis. They made this comment on the use of drawings in research with children:

> The use of drawings in collecting data from children shows that this is a valuable research tool. From a methodological point of view, this research makes a contribution to developing techniques for research on and with children within the developing discipline of 'children's studies'.
> (p.1033)

Visual analogues

Visual analogues are used by researchers to gain insight into experiences or feelings which children find hard to describe. 'Face scales' have been used to facilitate children's reports of their emotions and also experiences of pain (e.g. Le Baron and Zeltzer, 1984; McGrath *et al.*, 1985; West and Sammons, 1991; Ross *et al.*, 1993). Research into the quality of life for children with asthma asked children to colour in histograms (Christie *et al.*, 1993). In themselves, these sorts of techniques do not provide any in-depth information although they do increase the interactive nature of the research interview and can be used to facilitate discussion. Visual analogues are therefore best used as one of a number of approaches to obtaining information from a child (e.g. LeBaron and Zeltzer, 1984).

Play interviews

Play interviews refers to a particular technique developed by Erikson in the late 1950s (Erikson, 1958). They were used to explore a particular issue, and their use requires skills in interpreting children's play. The purpose of Erikson's study was to explore four year old children's feelings and experiences of hospitalisation. The children were 'interviewed' at least twice, with the 'interviews' consisting of the researcher observing a child playing with a bag of hospital-related toys. There was minimal interaction between the child and the researcher, and the child's narrative and actions were recorded. These were later coded, according to a Freudian framework, into patterns of play which indicated children's concerns. This technique has been used since, again with hospitalised children but also acutely ill and healthy children, to explore differences in the concerns of these different groups of children (Ritchie *et al.*, 1984).

Semi-projective techniques

Semi-projective techniques are especially useful in two particular research contexts; first, when the research demands information which either may be difficult for a child to reveal or talk about in terms of their own personal experience; and secondly, when the research seeks to discover underlying beliefs which a child or young person might find difficult to access or express verbally (Cassidy, 1988; McGurk and Glachan, 1988).

Lentz (1985) used a semi-projective approach to explore the fears and worries of five and six year old children known as *contextual play research*. In Lentz's study the research interview took place in a play setting, including two dolls' houses (representing the child's home and the babysitter's house), a school room, and dolls representing a little boy or girl, family members, teachers, other adults and children. The children played out a number of activities (e.g. going to bed, being left at the babysitter's) with the dolls and the researcher, and were asked what the little boy or girl was afraid or worried about. Contextual play research is, Lentz argues, an under-utilised research technique. She states:

> The usefulness of the particular method certainly does not end with investigations of fears and worries. The possibilities are virtually endless, and new realms of understanding young children may be opened... The creativity and insight of researchers are the only limiting factors.
> (Lentz, 1985, p. 987)

A more recent study into the fears and worries of young children also used semi-projective techniques (Stevenson-Hinde and Shouldice, 1995). In this study the children were given a *hand puppet* and asked to answer, on the puppet's behalf, questions addressed to the puppet by the researcher. The authors maintain that the quality of information they collected demonstrates that children find this technique far less threatening than direct questioning.

The *narrative story stem technique* was developed for work with children who had been maltreated (e.g. Bretherton *et al.*, 1990; Buchsbaum and Emde, 1990; Buchsbaum *et al.*, 1992). Again using dolls, the child is asked to play out the end of a series of stories introduced by the researchers in order to explore the family relationships of maltreated and non-maltreated children. Interpretation of the child's verbal and non-verbal responses is based on social-cognitive theories on the development of social knowledge (e.g. Smetana, 1983). As with other researchers using semi-projective techniques, Buchsbaum *et al.* (1992) believe that the narrative story stem technique offers a way into exploring, in a non-threatening way, the inner world of the child:

> We believe the story stem play narrative technique holds promise for both researchers and clinicians. ... We believe the narratives provide an opportunity to capture the child's representations of his or her world as they play out real-life themes.
> (p.616-617)

For older children, the use of dolls or puppets may be inappropriate. However, the technique of asking children to report feelings or experiences on behalf of an imaginary child, or in the third person, can help to overcome problems of shame or embarrassment when talking about sensitive issues.

Where the child is old enough to have sufficient skills, *drawing and writing* may be an appropriate technique. For young children, a more suitable approach may be to ask the child to dictate an account to the researcher, rather than ask them to write it down (e.g. Wenestam and Wass, 1987). As with other techniques, when drawings and writing are being used as a semi-projective method, then the research must be grounded in a clear theoretical approach which informs the interpretation and analysis of the data. Drawings offer a means of accessing beliefs, attitudes and conceptions of the world. Researchers have used drawings to explore children's attitudes towards teachers (Welsh *et al.*, 1971; Klepsch, 1979), health professionals (e.g. Klepsch and Logie, 1982), people with mental illness (Poster *et al.*, 1986) and health care (Phillips, 1980). They have also been used to explore self-concept among children with cranio-facial abnormalities (e.g. LeFebvre and Munro, 1978); and healthy and dying children's concepts of death (e.g. Spinetta and Deasy-Spinetta, 1981; Lansdown and Benjamin, 1985; Wenestam and Wass, 1987; Clunies-Ross and Lansdown, 1988; Tamm and Granqvist, 1995).

Children with communication or learning difficulties

The principles of research outlined in the previous two sections apply to all disabled children and young people. However, research with children with communication or learning difficulties presents additional challenges.

> Experimentation and risk-taking become important, because we need to develop ways to talk and interact with individuals who have intellectual deficits that do not place them in a lesser position. ... The dependence of the qualitative researcher on language and the image of the ideal informant as an articulate person, may call for some creative tactics in the face of an informant who cannot verbally inform.
> (Biklen and Moseley, 1988, p.161)

This section collates reports from researchers about techniques which ensure that these children are given a voice. In addition, the reader is referred to Marchant and Page's (1992) report. Although it concerns child protection work with children with multiple disabilities, it contains information which is pertinent to research interviews as well.

The techniques which researchers have developed in order that people with learning and/or communication difficulties can participate in research have often been highly innovative and experimental (Minkes *et al.*,

1994). It is often difficult to know which aspects of a particular methodology 'worked' in terms of facilitating communication between the researcher and the interviewee (Robinson, 1995). There is a pressing need for evaluation of these various techniques. Furthermore, funders need to acknowledge that research with people with learning and/or communication difficulties will make additional demands on a project's budget, both in terms of the need for extra time in the field for pilot work and data collection, as well as for developing special resources or aides.

> The decision to involve people with mental handicaps in the research design, and actively to seek their viewpoints and personal experiences, is easy to justify. Ways need to be found, however, of enabling people with mental handicaps to take part in this process. ... It means investing time in personal contact and, within the context of a relationship, allowing the full picture of a person to emerge. In a generously resourced research project which allows frequent, regular, and close contact between researchers and respondents over a long period, and which employs a range of opportunities for conversation and observation, many research problems can be overcome.
> (Atkinson, 1988, p.76)

The need for extended contact

To understand the experiences and perspectives of people with severe learning difficulties takes time because the impairment initially prevents the researcher seeing the individual (Goode, 1984). A number of researchers advocate a naturalistic approach involving observation and conversation over a prolonged period of time (e.g. Edgerton, 1984; Atkinson, 1988; Barnes, 1992).

> It is important for the qualitative researcher who wants to learn about the worlds of subjects with severe mental retardation to supplement information received through verbal discussions with observations in the places where they live and work.
> (Biklen and Moseley, 1988, p.161)

With respect to children, this approach has been adopted, to some extent, in research into disabled children in the school context (Wade and Moore, 1993).

Many projects, however, do not have the funding which allows such long-term work. Instead, the researcher has to rely on individual interviews. The remainder of this section therefore considers ways to facilitate interviews with children with learning and/or communication difficulties. However, it is worth reiterating once more the need to spend as much time as possible developing rapport with the interviewee, ensuring that they fully understand the nature of the research, and obtaining informed consent (Flynn, 1986; Roberts et al., 1988).

The type of question

It is important that questions are specific and concrete (Biklen and Moseley, 1988; Nugent and Faucette, 1995). Complex or abstract questions will need to be broken down into more specific items.

> Most qualitative researchers are trained to ask open-ended questions in order to allow respondents to frame answers from their own perspectives.

When interviewing persons with severe mental retardation, however, such questions may become more confusing than clarifying. ...Break requests for information into parts and ask separate questions about each.
(Biklen and Moseley, 1988, p.158)

Where it is necessary to 'break down' questions, it is crucial that the researcher is vigilant about the possibility of the questions reflecting his or own concerns or assumptions, rather than those of the interviewee. In order to overcome this particular problem, Moseley (1988) recommended extensive observational work prior to conducting interviews.

An indication of the level at which questions should be phrased will be gained from spending time with the interviewee prior to the research interview or during the time spent building up rapport. In addition, observing how people who know the interviewees interact with them will also give some idea of verbal or communicative ability and the need to modify pace or enunciation (Roberts *et al.*, 1988). If the interviewee is unable to answer the question, then it is important that the interviewer rephrases the question (Flynn, 1986).

As with very young children, people with learning difficulties often have difficulty answering questions which relate to time or frequency (Biklen and Moseley, 1988; Flynn, 1986; Roberts *et al.*, 1988). In addition, their reasoning abilities may be limited. For example, although they have a definite preference, they may not be able to explain why they are happier in one environment compared to another (People First, 1994).

Reducing demand on verbal abilities

Many children who have difficulty speaking use *symbol boards* (e.g. Bliss, Makaton, Rebus) as their means of communication though their usefulness is limited by the vocabulary or symbols which are included. It is possible, however, to develop a symbol board, or incorporate symbols onto an existing board, which includes the words or vocabulary pertinent to a research or clinical issue. This was done successfully by Marchant and Page (1992) for their clinical investigative interviews with possible victims of abuse.

Pictures and photographs are often used in research with children and young people with learning and/or communication difficulties. A number of researchers have found that they increase responsiveness (Roberts *et al.*, 1988; March, 1992; Minkes *et al.*, 1994) as well as reduce the demands made on verbal abilities. The simultaneous presentation of a number of pictures or photographs also reduces response bias (March, 1992). The *smiley face scale* has been used by a number of researchers to ascertain individuals' feelings about particular issues (e.g. Roberts *et al.*, 1988; Booth *et al.*, 1990; People First, 1994). Researchers at the Norah Fry Research Centre have developed an alternative to the smiley face scale (Robinson, 1995). This consists of three pictures: a thumb pointing up, a thumb pointing down and a thumb half way between. There are a number of ways in which the interviewee can express his or her choice. They can point to, or pick up, the appropriate picture or a 'postbox' can be used (e.g. Booth *et al.*, 1990).

Finally, verbal or communicative abilities may prohibit the use of certain research techniques especially group discussions (People First, 1994; Robinson, 1995).

Non-verbal communication

A number of researchers point to the importance of noting, and later recording, non-verbal behaviour during the research interview (e.g. Flynn, 1986; Roberts *et al.*, 1988; Robinson, 1995). Flynn (1986) advocates making detailed field notes straight after an interview for use in conjunction with the interview transcripts during the analytical stage. The researcher should not assume, however, that they can correctly interpret informal gestures, facial expressions and body language (Puddicombe, 1995). This is especially the case when the interviewee has some form of motor impairment. The researcher may therefore need the assistance of a familiar person to help them interpret non-verbal communication (see below).

A familiar context

A familiar setting for the research interview is particularly important for children with learning difficulties (Marchant and Page, 1992). Unfamiliar environments, including the unfamiliar face of the interviewer, can be both inhibiting and highly distracting (Minkes *et al.*, 1994).

Involving a familiar person in the research interview

There are a number of reasons why it may be appropriate to involve a familiar person in the research interview, either as the interviewer or as an interpreter. Such a person can assist the researcher in understanding the informant's language and methods of communication. They can also provide personal information which enables the researcher to make sense of the interviewee's responses (Roberts *et al.*, 1988; Gold,

1994; Minkes *et al.*, 1994). Finally, they can act to reassure the interviewee.

Despite the advantages of using a familiar person, there are distinct drawbacks of which the researcher needs to be aware. First, the familiar person may inhibit the interviewee's responses, especially if the research is connected in some way to that person. Secondly, the familiar person may act, 'not just as a translator, but as a filter as well' (Biklen and Moseley, 1988, p.159; see also Minkes *et al.*, 1994). That is, the informant's responses will be translated according to the familiar person's perspective. Providing sufficient training in interviewing or interpreting skills can help to overcome these problems, and is a necessary pre-requisite to involving additional people in a research interview (Minkes *et al.*, 1994).

Increasing involvement of children in the whole research process

The involvement of children in research beyond that of being research subjects remains very limited. However, a number of recently published studies have consulted with children early on in research projects. Typically this has involved group discussions with children and adolescents to inform the content of questionnaires and interview schedules (eg. Roberts *et al.*, 1988; Telfair *et al.*, 1994). Involvement of children at a more general level, such as during the stages of developing research agendas and formulating proposals, is still lacking. In this penultimate section, we consider ways which will promote greater involvement of children, including disabled children, in the whole research process.

It is necessary to turn to other fields of research for examples of increased 'user involvement' in research. Tozer and Thornton's (1995) report on the workings of an older people's research advisory group is a particularly good example. The Norah Fry Research Centre at the University of Bristol has a permanent group of adults with learning disabilities who act as a user research advisory group. Their brief extends beyond advising on particular projects to being involved in thinking about and planning future research projects. Some research funders (for example, the Joseph Rowntree Foundation, the Economic and Social Research Council) are also encouraging, and providing funds to cover the costs of, consulting with representatives of research populations. The form of this input must, however, be flexible. Although formal meetings may be familiar and non-threatening to researchers and practitioners, they may not necessarily be the most acceptable or effective way of consulting with children and young people (Cavet, 1996).

It is, however, from the field of research with disabled adults that the most useful models of participation can be gleaned. An earlier section of this review has described how disabled people, including disabled researchers, have long called for greater empowerment to disabled people within the research process. Zarb (1992) defined four key questions which can be used to evaluate the way research is conducted. Although he is referring to disabled adults, the principles equally apply to children, including those with disabilities.

> There are a number of important questions which can be used as a starting point for the critical evaluation of existing research:
>
> i.   Who controls what the research will be about and how it will be carried out?
>
> ii.   How far have we come in involving disabled people in the research process?
>
> iii. What opportunities exist for disabled people to criticise the research and influence future directions?
>
> iv.   What happens to the products of the research?
>
> (Zarb, 1992, p.128)

There are a few examples of the way these principles have been put into practice. A study of the experiences of people with learning disabilities moving from long-stay institutions into community homes demonstrates some of the ways these principles can be applied (People First, 1994). This project, funded by the Joseph Rowntree Foundation, was carried out jointly by a researcher from the King's Fund Centre, who was called the project supporter, and an advocacy group for people with learning difficulties known as People First. The interviews were carried out by members of People First. They also worked with the project supporter in the analysis of the material. The output from the research included a simply worded summary of the research findings (written by the interviewers), a full research report, a tape summarising the findings, and a separate report on how the study was carried out. The National Development Team have also been innovative in working with adults with learning difficulties throughout the research process. They consulted with a self-advocacy group of adults with learning difficulties about carrying out a survey of respite services; some members of this group were then involved in analysing and writing a summary of research findings (Flynn *et al.*, 1995).

Instances of using representatives from the research population to conduct interviews can also be found in research with children. Barnardos have recently completed a couple of projects in which children and young people interviewed other children or young people. One of these projects concerned issues related to mainstream education of disabled children, and disabled adolescents interviewed disabled and non-disabled peers (Ash *et al.*, 1996). Adult researchers oversaw the project and were responsible for carrying out the data analysis and report writing.

Deaf people have also tended to be more involved in the research process than other groups. A video jointly produced by a hearing researcher and a deaf researcher on doing research with deaf people (Jones and Pullen, 1995) points out that there are two reasons why it is important to involve deaf people in the research process. First, there is the need for someone with signing skills to carry out interviews with deaf people. Secondly, deaf people identify themselves strongly as a separate cultural group - and this must be accounted for throughout the whole research process.

There are also pockets of good practice in relation to dissemination of research findings, and some funders have clearly recognised the need for a number of 'levels' of dissemination (Hurst, 1991; Economic and Social Research Council, 1992). Bashford *et al.* (1995) report an interesting development at the Norah Fry Research Centre at the University of Bristol. The Centre, which carries out research with people with learning difficulties, has been experimenting with the idea of 'parallel texts'. Basically this involves producing a research report and a parallel text in simplified language which can be used by people with learning difficulties. Given the enormous range of ability of people with learning difficulties, the original and simplified versions are integrated as closely as possible so that the simplified version can be used to provide access to the original text. Though not prescriptive, Bashford *et al.* offer a number of guidelines to writing parallel texts. This includes suggestions about sentence construction, vocabulary, using 'real-life' examples to illustrate findings. They also point to the importance of presentation, including the size of the text, print style and use of headings and illustrations. Finally, the authors recommend the use of potential readers as consultant editors as early possible in the writing process.

> People with intellectual disabilities will often have strong ideas about what they want to get out of a document and it is important to listen to what they can tell us about presenting material in accessible forms.
>
> (Bashford *et al.*, 1995, p. 218)

It is important to emphasise here that empowering research subjects and representatives from research populations has significant cost implications (Barnes, 1992). Dissemination costs will be higher, especially if a number of different media are used, such as videos, tape recordings or CD-Roms. There are also costs related to consulting and involving research subjects throughout the research process. Finally, it is worth noting that it is now quite common to find that children involved in research receive some form of payment. This payment is not regarded as an inducement to take part in the research, but rather as an indication of the value placed by the researchers on the child or young person's views or opinions (Alderson, 1995).

Conclusion

Giving precedence to the views and opinions of disabled children in research on childhood disability offers a number of challenges to researchers. It requires a 're-working' of the way we view children, and of the way we do research. This review has considered the reasoning which establishes the necessity of taking such a new approach to research on childhood disability. At a more practical level, it has also provided an overview of the types of method which appear to be most suitable for including disabled children in research that concerns their lives. Throughout we have emphasised the importance of working in partnership with children in the research process. We hope that it contributes, in some way, to ensuring that the voices of disabled children are truly heard.

The review was carried out when the need to conduct research *with disabled children*, as opposed to research *on childhood disability*, was increasingly acknowledged. It does not claim to be comprehensive because research that directly involves children, both disabled and non-disabled, is such a rapidly developing field. New ideas and new approaches are being developed all the time. In this situation it is important that researchers share information, both to avoid re-inventing the wheel and to ensure that children are not exposed to methods which have already proved unsuccessful. We should, then, devote more attention to describing *fully* the research methods used when publishing research findings, and especially to details of what *did* and *did not* work well. Children have an important role to play in evaluating research approaches and their assessments, favourable and unfavourable, should be included in published accounts of research methods.

Research *with* disabled children means more than having children as 'research subjects', and using 'child-friendly' research methods. Although a substantial part of our paper has focused on methodology, this should not detract from the importance of working with disabled children throughout the *whole* research process. A key message from the review is that disabled children need to be empowered by their involvement with research: they need to be consulted about research priorities and research design, involved in analysis and writing, and should receive an accessible version of the research report. While we could find few examples of disabled children being fully engaged in the research process, some of the research techniques we have described clearly have a potential use during the consultative phases of that process. Again it is important that researchers share their experiences of these 'hidden' stages of a research project. It is only by drawing attention to these aspects of research that they will become accepted as necessary to research, and likewise more acceptable to bodies and institutions who fund research of this kind.

There are clearly a number of implications arising from our discussion of methodological and ethical issues which will need to be considered in the commissioning and funding of research. First, such research requires a commitment to including children whose disabilities challenge conventional research methodologies. A more eclectic approach to methods, and the willingness and time to experiment and obtain feedback from children will be needed. Secondly, there needs to be careful consideration of recruitment methods, and the ways in which information about a study can be conveyed to children and their informed assent obtained. Thirdly, such research should not be planned in isolation from the views of children themselves. Consultation with children at the outset should ensure that their views of the important issues are represented. Fourthly, researchers may need to set up support systems that can be mobilised if concerns raised by a child indicate the need for more ongoing support. Finally, it is important that, where possible, children are involved in presenting the findings of research, and different ways of doing so will be needed for different audiences, including disabled children. All such material, whether written, on video or audiocassette, pictorial or verbal, should be professionally and attractively presented, thus conveying the value attached to the children's views. Research that truly engages disabled children themselves is likely to be labour intensive and relatively expensive, but we hope that this will not deter funding bodies from commissioning good quality research.

The issues of involvement and consultation do not only concern researchers. Current policies in a number of areas highlight the importance of obtaining users' views. So far, however, there is little evidence that disabled children are being consulted about the services they use. It has been suggested that one of the reasons for failing to access their views is that 'not all services understand that disabled children can express a view about their future, nor that they may know most about their condition or their preferred support services or treatments' (Russell, 1995, p.54). Our review demonstrates that it is possible to find credible, and acceptable, ways of doing this. The task now is to continue to develop and improve research with disabled children, and then to disseminate the resulting information – both about children's views and about reliable methods to obtain such views – so that agencies can work towards developing services that fully meet the needs of disabled children.

References

ALDERSON, P. (1995) *Listening to Children: Children, Ethics and Social Research*, London: Barnardos.

ALDERSON, P. and MAYALL, B. (eds) (1994) *Children's Decisions in Health Care and Research*, Report of the SSRU Consent Conference Series Number 5, London: Social Science Research Unit, University of London.

AMBERT, A.M. (1986) 'Sociology of Sociology: the place of children in North American sociology', in ALDER, P.A. and ALDER, P. (eds) *Sociological Studies of Child Development*, 1, Greenwich, Connecticut: JAI Press.

ASH, A., BELLEW, J., DAVIES, M., NEWMAN, T. and RICHARDSON, L. (1996) *Everybody in?*, Barkingside: Barnardos.

ATKINSON, D. (1988) 'Research interviews with people with mental handicaps', *Mental Handicap Research*, 1, 1, 75-90.

BACKETT, K. and ALEXANDER, H. (1991) 'Talking to young children about health: methods and findings', *Health Education Journal*, 50, 1, 34-38.

BARNES, C. (1992) 'Qualitative research: valuable or irrelevant?', *Disability, Handicap & Society*, 7, 2, 115-123.

BASCH, C. (1987) 'Focus group interview: an underutilised research technique for improving theory and practice in health education', *Health Education Quarterly*, 14, 441-448.

BASHFORD, L., TOWNSLEY, R. and WILLIAMS, C. (1995) 'Parallel text: making research accessible to people with intellectual disabilities', *International Journal of Disability, Development and Education*, 42, 3, 211-220.

BEARISON, D.J. (1991) *'They Never Want to Tell You': children talk about cancer*, Cambridge, Massachusetts: Harvard University Press.

BECKER, H. (1966/7) 'Whose side are we on?', *Social Problems*, 14, 239-247.

BERESFORD, B. (1992) *Coping with Epilepsy in Childhood: an examination in factors mediating adjustment in children with epilepsy*, Unpublished PhD thesis, University of Exeter.

BERRY, S., HAYFORD, J., ROSS, C., PACHMAN, L. and LAVIGNE, J. (1993) 'Conceptions of illness by children with juvenile rheumatoid arthritis: a cognitive developmental approach', *Journal of Pediatric Psychology*, 18, 83-97.

BERSOFF, D. and HOFER, P. (1990) 'The legal regulation of school psychology', in GUTKIN, T. and REYNOLDS, C. (eds) *The Handbook of Social Psychology*, (2nd edition), New York: Wiley.

BIKLEN, S.K. and MOSELEY, C.R. (1988) '"Are you retarded?" "No, I'm catholic": qualitative methods in the study of people with severe handicaps', *Journal of the Association for Persons with Severe Handicaps*, 13, 155-162.

BILLINGS, A.G., MOOS, R.H., MILLER, J.J. and GOTTLIEB, J.E. (1987) 'Psychosocial adaptation in juvenile rheumatic disease: a controlled evaluation', *Health Psychology*, 6, 4, 343-359.

BOGDAN, R. and TAYLOR, S. (1976) 'The judged, not the judges', *American Psychologist*, 47-52.

BONE, M. and MELTZER, H. (1989) *The Prevalence of Disability Among Children*, London: HMSO.

BOOTH, T. and BOOTH, W. (1994) 'The use of depth interviewing with vulnerable subjects: lessons from a research study of parents with learning disabilities', *Social Science and Medicine*, 39, 3, 415-424.

BOOTH, T., SIMONS, K. and BOOTH, W. (1990) *Outward Bound: relocation and community care for people with learning difficulties*, Milton Keynes: Open University Press.

BRANNEN, J. and O'BRIEN, M. (1995) 'Childhood and the sociological gaze: paradigms and paradoxes', *Sociology*, 4, 729-737.

BRETHERTON, I., RIDGEWAY, D. and CASSIDY, J. (1990) 'The role of internal working models in the attachment relationship', in GREENBERG, M., CICCHETTI, D. and CUMMINGS, E.M. (eds)

Attachment during the pre-school years, Chicago: Chicago University Press.

BREWSTER, A. (1982) 'Chronically ill hospitalized children's concepts of their illness', *Pediatrics*, 69, 355-362.

BRITISH PAEDIATRIC ASSOCIATION (Ethics Advisory Committee) (1992) *Guidelines for the Ethical Conduct of Medical Research Involving Children*, London: British Paediatric Association.

BRITISH PSYCHOLOGICAL SOCIETY (1991) *Revised Ethical Principles for Constructing Research with Human Participants*, Leicester: British Psychological Society.

BRITISH SOCIOLOGICAL ASSOCIATION (1993) *Guidelines for Good Professional Conduct and Statement of Ethical Practice*, London: British Sociological Association.

BRODIN, J. (1993) 'Children and adolescents with brittle bones – psychosocial aspects', *Child: care, health and development*, 19, 341-347.

BRONFENBRENNER, U. (1979) *The Ecology of Human Development*, Harvard University Press: Massachusetts: Cambridge.

BUCHSBAUM, H.K. and EMDE, R.N. (1990) 'Play narratives in 36 month-old children: early moral development and family relationships', *Psychoanalytic Study of the Child*, 45, 129-155.

BUSCHBAUM, H.K., TOTH, S.L., CLYMAN, R.B., CICCHETTI, D. and EMDE, R.N. (1992) 'The use of a narrative story stem technique with maltreated children: implications for theory and practice', *Development and Psychopathology*, 4, 603-625.

CASSIDY, J. (1988) 'Child-mother attachments and the self in six year olds', *Child Development*, 59, 121-124.

CAVET, J. (1996) *Personal Communication*, University of Staffordshire, Stafford.

CHESTON, R. (1994) 'The accounts of special education leavers', *Disability and Society*, 9, 1, 59-69.

Children Act (1989), London: HMSO.

Children (Scotland) Act (1995), Edinburgh: HMSO.

CHISHOLM, L. (1990) 'Action research: some methodological and political considerations', *British Educational Research Journal*, 16, 3, 249-257

CHRISTIE, M.J., FRENCH, D., SOWDEN, A. and WEST, A. (1993) 'Development of child-centered disease-specific questionnaires for living with asthma', *Psychosomatic Medicine*, 55, 6, 541-548.

CLAFLIN, C. and BARBARIN, O. (1991) 'Does "telling" less protect more? Relationships among age, information disclosure, and what children with cancer see and feel', *Journal of Pediatric Psychology*, 16, 161-191.

CLUNIES-ROSS, C. and LANSDOWN, R. (1988) 'Concepts of death, illness and isolation found in children with leukaemia', *Child: care, health and development*, 14, 373-386.

COMMITTEE ON THE RIGHTS OF THE CHILD, Eighth Session, January 1995 *Consideration of Reports Submitted by States' Parties Under Article 44 of the Convention. Concluding Observations: United Kingdom of Great Britain and Northern Ireland*, United Nations Committee on the Rights of the Child.

Convention on the Rights of the Child: adopted by the General Assembly of the United Nations on 20 November 1989, London: HMSO.

CURRY, S. and RUSS, S. (1985) 'Identifying coping strategies in children', *Journal of Clinical Child Psychology*, 14, 61-69.

DiLEO, F. (1970) *Young Children and Their Drawing*, New York: Brunner/Mazel.

ECONOMIC AND SOCIAL RESEARCH COUNCIL (ESRC) (1992) 'New communication and evaluation policies', *Social Sciences - News from the ESRC*, 17, 6.

EDGERTON, R.B. (ed) (1984) *Lives In Process: mildly retarded adults in a large city, Monograph 6*, Washington DC: AAMD.

EISER, C. (1990) *Chronic Childhood Disease: An Introduction to Psychological Theory and Research*, Cambridge: Cambridge University Press.

EISER, C., EISER, J.R. and JONES, B.A. (1990) 'Scene schemata and scripts in children's understanding of hospital', *Child: care, health and development*, 16, 303-317.

EISER, C., HAVERMANS, T., CRAFT, A. and KERNAHAN, J. (1995) 'Development of a measure to assess the perceived illness experience after treatment for cancer', *Archives of Disease in Childhood*, 72, 302-307.

ENNETT, S.T., DeVELLIS, B.M., EARP, J.A., KREDICH, D., WARREN, R.W. and WILHELM, C.L. (1991) 'Disease experience and psychosocial adjustment in children with juvenile rheumatoid arthritis: children's versus mothers' reports', *Journal of Pediatric Psychology*, 16, 5, 557-568.

ERIKSON, F.H. (1958) *Play Interviews for Four-Year-Old Hospitalized Children*, Monographs of the Society for Research in Childhood Development, Inc., Vol. XXIII, Serial No. 69, No 3, Indiana: Child Development Publications.

Family Law Reform Act (1969), London: HMSO.

FEATHERSTONE, H. (1980) *A Difference in the Family*, New York: Basic Books.

FERGUSON, P., FERGUSON, D. and TAYLOR, S. (1992a) 'Introduction: interpretivism and disability studies', in FERGUSON, P., FERGUSON, D. and TAYLOR, S. (eds) *Interpreting Disability: a qualitative reader*, New York: Teachers College Press.

FERGUSON, P., FERGUSON, D. and TAYLOR, S. (1992b) 'Conclusion: the future of interpretivism in disability studies', in FERGUSON, P., FERGUSON, D. and TAYLOR, S. (eds) *Interpreting Disability: a qualitative reader*, New York: Teachers College Press.

FESTERVAND, T. (1984-1985) 'An introduction and application of focus group research to the health care industry', *Health Marketing Quarterly*, 2, (2-3), 199-209.

FINE, G.A. and SANDSTROM, K.L. (1988) *Knowing Children: participant observation with minors*, Qualitative Research Methods Series, Volume 15, Newbury Park, California: Sage.

FIVUSH, R., GRAY, J.T. and FROMHOFF, F.A. (1987) 'Two-year olds talk about the past', *Cognitive development*, 2, 393-409.

FLYNN, M. (1986) 'Adults who are mentally handicapped as consumers: issues and guidelines for interviewing', *Journal of Mental Deficiency Research*, 30, 369-377.

FLYNN, M., COTTERILL, L., HAYES, L. and SLOPER, T. (1995) *A Break with Tradition: the findings of a survey of respite services for adult citizens with learning disabilities in England*, Manchester: National Development Team.

FOLCH-LYON, E. and TROST, J. (1981) 'Conducting focus group discussions', *Studies in Family Planning*, 12, 12, 443-449.

FORMAN, E. and LADD, R. (1991) *Ethical dilemnas in pediatrics: a case study approach*, New York: Springer-Verlagg.

GERBER, D.A. (1990) 'Listening to disabled people: the problem of voice and authority in Robert B. Edgerton's "The Cloak of Competence"', *Disability, Handicap and Society*, 5, 1, 3-23.

Gillick v. West Norfolk and Wisbech AHA. [1984]1 All ER 373.

Gillick v. Wisbech & West Norfolk AHA. [1985] 3 All ER 423.

GOLD, D. (1994) '"We don't call it a circle": the ethos of a support group', *Disability and Society*, 9, 4, 435-452.

GOFFMAN, E. (1961) *Asylums*, Harmondsworth: Penguin.

GOODE, D. (1984) 'Socially produced identities, intimacy and the problem of competence among the retarded', in BARTON, L. and TOMLINSON, S. (eds) *Special Education and Social Interests*, New York: Nichols.

GOODE, D. (1986) 'Kids, culture and innocents', *Human Studies*, 9, 83-106.

GOODENOUGH, F. (1926) *Measurement of Intelligence by Drawings*, New York: World Book Company.

GREENFIELD, J. (1970) *A Child Called Noah*, New York: Holt, Rinehart and Winston.

HAVERMANS, T. and EISER, C. (1994) 'Siblings of a child with cancer', *Child: care, health and development*, 20, 309-322.

HOPPE, M.J., WELLS, E.A., MORRISON, D.M., GILLMORE, M.R. and WILSDON, A. (1995) 'Using focus groups to discuss sensitive topics with children', *Evaluation Review*, 19, 1, 102-114.

HUBERT, N., JAY, S., SALTOUN, M. and HAYES, M. (1988) 'Approach-avoidance and distress in children undergoing preparation for painful medical procedures', *Journal of Clinical Child Psychology*, 17, 194-202.

HURST, R. (1991) *Drafting Findings*, York: Joseph Rowntree Foundation.

JONES, L. and PULLEN, G. (1995) *Everything you have wanted to know about deaf people but didn't know how to ask*, A Videotaped Guide to Deaf People's Participation in Research, Social Policy Research Unit, University of York.

KALNINS, I., McQUEEN, D.V., BACKETT, K.C., CURTICE, L. and CURRIE, C.C. (1992) 'Children, empowerment and health promotion: some new directions in research and practice', *Health Promotion International*, 7, 1, 53-59.

KATZ, E., KELLERMAN, J. and SIEGEL, S. (1980) 'Behavioral distress in children with cancer undergoing medical procedures: developmental considerations, *Journal of Consulting and Clinical Psychology*, 48, 356-365.

KEITH-SPIEGAL, P. (1983) 'Children and consent to participate in research', in MELTON, G., KOOCHER, G.

and SAKS, M. (eds) *Children's competence to consent*, New York: Plenum.

KINARD, E. (1985) 'Ethical issues in research with abused children', *Child Abuse and Neglect*, 9, 301-311.

KLEPSCH, M. (1979) *A validation study of the draw-a-teacher technique on third grade children*, Unpublished doctoral dissertation, University of North Colorado.

KLEPSCH, M. and LOGIE, L. (1982) *Children Draw and Tell: an introduction to the projective uses of children's human figure drawings*, New York: Bruner/Mazel.

KOOCHER, G.P. (1981) 'Children's conceptions of death', in BIBACE, R. and WALSH, M. (eds) *Children's Conceptions of Health, Illness and Bodily Function*, New Directions for Child Development. No. 14, San Francisco: Jossey-Bass.

KOOCHER, G. and KEITH-SPIEGEL, P. (1994) 'Scientific issues on psychosocial and educational research with children', in GRODIN, M.A. and GLANTZ, L.H. (eds) *Children as Research Subjects: science, ethics and law*, New York: Oxford University Press.

KRAHN, G.L., HOHN, M.F. and KIME, C. (1995) 'Incorporating qualitative approaches into clinical child psychology research', *Journal of Clinical Child Psychology*, 24, 2, 204-213.

KRUEGER, R. (1988) *Focus Groups: A Practical Guide for Applied Research*, Newbury Park, CA: Sage.

LANSDOWN, R. and BENJAMIN, G. (1985) 'The development of the concept of death in children aged 5–9 years', *Child: care, health and development*, 11, 13-20.

LAUROUL, J. (1995) *Personal communication*, Norah Fry Research Centre, University of Bristol.

Le BARON, S. and ZELTZER, L. (1984) 'Assessment of acute pain and anxiety on children and adolescents by self-reports, observer reports and a behavioural checklist', *Journal of Consulting and Clinical Psychology*, 52, 5, 729-738.

LeFEBVRE, A. and MUNRO, I. (1978) 'The role of psychiatry in a craniofacial team', *Plastic and Reconstructive Surgery*, 61, 564-569.

LENTZ, K. (1985) 'Fears and worries of young children as expressed in a contextual play setting', *Journal of Child Psychology and Psychiatry*, 26, 6, 981-987.

LEVIN, I. (1994) 'Children's perceptions of their family', in BRANNEN, J. and O'BRIEN (eds) *Childhood and Parenthood: proceedings of the International Sociological Association Committee for Family Research Conference*, Institute of Education, London: University of London.

MacDONALD, W. and TOPPER, G. (1989) 'Focus-group research with children: a structural approach', *Applied Marketing Research*, 28, 2, 3-11.

MACKAY, R. (1991) 'Conceptions of children and models of socialisation', in WAKSLER, F. (ed) *Studying the Social Worlds of Children: sociological readings*, London: The Falmer Press.

MAHON, A., GLENDINNING, C. and CLARKE, K. (1995) 'Reflections on researching children: some methodological issues', *Paper given on the Medical Sociology section of the British Sociological Association's annual conference*, University of York, September 1995.

MANDELL, N. (1988) 'The least-adult role in studying children', *Journal of Contemporary Ethnography*, 16, 4, 433-467.

MARCH, P. (1992) 'Do photographs help adults with severe mental handicaps to make choices?', *The British Journal of Mental Subnormality*, 28, 2, 122-128.

MARCHANT, R. and PAGE, M. (1992) *Bridging the Gap: child protection work with children with multiple disabilities*, London: NSPCC.

MARTIN, J., MELTZER, H. and ELLIOTT, D. (1988) *The Prevalence of Disability Among Adults*, London: HMSO.

MATES, D. and ALLISON, K.R. (1992) 'Sources of stress and coping responses of high school students', *Adolescence*, 27, 106, 461-474.

McGRATH, P.J., JOHNSON, G., GOODMAN, J., SCHILLINGER, J., DUNN, J. and CHAPMAN, J. (1985) 'The CHEOPS: a behavioural scale to measure post operative pain in children', in FIELDS, H., DUBNER, R. and CEVERO, F. (eds) *Advances in Pain Research and Therapy*, New York: Raven Press.

McGURK, H. and GLACHAN, M. (1988) 'Children's conversation with adults', *Children and Society*, 2, 1, 20-34.

MEDICAL RESEARCH COUNCIL (1991) *The Ethical Conduct of Research on Children*, London: Medical Research Council.

MENKE, E.M. (1987) 'The impact of a child's chronic illness on school-aged siblings', *Children's Health Care*, 15, 132-140.

MILLDE, K. (1990) *Adolescents with brittle bones. Their everyday life and leisure*, The WRP Group, Handicap Research, University College of Jönköping, Sweden.

MILLDE, K. (ed) (1991) *Three adolescents tell their stories*, WRP International, Rockneby, Sweden.

MILLER, S., SHERMAN, H., COMBS, C. and KRUUS, L. (1992) 'Patterns of children's coping with short-term medical and dental stressors: nature, implications and future directions', in LaGRECA, A., SIEGEL, L., WALLNDER, J. and WALKER, C. (eds) *Stress and Coping in Child Health*, New York: The Guilford Press.

MINKES, J., ROBINSON, C. and WESTON, C. (1994) 'Consulting the Children: interviews with children using residential respite care services', *Disability and Society*, 9, 1, 47-57.

MORGAN, D. (1988) *Focus groups as qualitative research*, Qualitative Research Methods Series, Volume 16, Newbury Park, CA: Sage.

MOSELEY, C. (1988) *What Work Means: people with severe disabilities in the workplace*, Unpublished doctoral dissertation, Syracuse University, Syracruse.

MORROW, V. (1992) *A sociological study of the economic roles of children, with particular reference to Birmingham and Cambridge*, Unpublished PhD dissertation: Faculty and Social and Political Sciences, University of Cambridge.

NUGENT, P. and FAUCETTE, N. (1995) 'Marginalized voices: constructions of and responses to physical education and grading practices by students categorized as gifted or learning disabled', *Journal of Teaching in Physical Education*, 14, 4, 418-430.

OAKLEY, A., BENDELOW, G., BARNES, J., BUCHANAN, M. and HUSAIN, O.A.N. (1995) 'Health and cancer prevention: knowledge and beliefs of children and young people', *British Medical Journal*, 310, 1029-1033.

OLIVER, M. (1990) *The Politics of Disablement*, London: Macmillan.

OLIVER, M. (1992) 'Changing the social relations of research production?', *Disability, Handicap and Society*, 7, 2, 101-114.

OPIE, I. and OPIE, P. (1991) 'The culture of children', in WAKSLER, F.C. (ed) *Studying the Social Worlds of Children, Sociological Readings*, London: The Falmer Press.

PEOPLE FIRST (1994) *Outside but not inside.....yet!*, People First: London.

PHILLIPS, S. (1980) 'Children's perceptions of health and disease', *Canadian Family Physician*, 26, 1171-1174.

POSTER, E.C., BETZ, C., McKENNA, A. and MOSSAIR, M. (1986) 'Children's attitudes toward the mentally ill as reflected in human figure drawings and stories', *Journal of the American Academy of Child and Adolescent Psychiatry*, 25, 5, 680-686.

POWELL, M.P. and VACHA-HAASE, T. (1994) 'Issues related to research with children: what counselling psychologists need to know', *The Counselling Psychologist*, 22, 3, 444-453.

PROUT, A. and JAMES, A. (1990) 'A new paradigm for the sociology of childhood? Provenance, promise and problems', in JAMES, A. and PROUT, A. (eds) *Constructing and reconstructing childhood: contemporary issues in the sociological study of childhood*, London: The Falmer Press.

PUDDICOME, B. (1995) *Face to Face: communicating with people who do not use language*, London: Values into Action.

QVORTRUP, J. (1994a) 'Childhood and modern society: a paradoxical relationship', in BRANNEN, J. and O'BRIEN, M. (eds) *Childhood and Parenthood: proceedings of the International Sociological Association Committee for Family Research Conference 1994*, Institute of Education, University of London: London.

QVORTRUP, J. (1994b) 'Childhood Matters: an introduction', in QVORTRUP, J., BARDY, M., SIGRITTA, G. and WINTERSBERGER, H. (eds) *Childhood Matters: social theory, practice and politics*, Aldershot: Avebury.

RAVIV, D. and STONE, A. (1991) 'Individual differences in the self-image of adolescents with learning disabilities: the roles of severity, time of diagnosis, and parental perceptions', *Journal of Learning Disabilties*, 24, 10, 602-611.

REICH, P. (1986) *Language Development*, Englewood Cliffs, New Jersey: Prentice Hall.

RITALA-KOSKINEN, A. (1994) 'Children and the construction of close relationships: how to find out the children's point of view', in BRANNEN, J. and O'BRIEN, M. (eds) *Childhood and Parenthood: proceedings of the International Sociological Association Committee for Family Research Conference*, Institute of Education, University of London: London.

RITCHIE, J.A., CATY, S. and ELLERTON, M.L. (1984) 'Concerns of acutely ill, chronically ill, and healthy pre-school children', *Research in Nursing and Health*, 7, 4, 265-274.

ROBERTS, D., FLYNN, M. and HIRST, M. (1988) *Development and piloting of an interview schedule for use with young people with mental handicap*, Working Paper DHSS 483 10/88, Social Policy Research Unit: University of York.

ROBINSON, G. (1995) *Personal Communication*, Norah Fry Research Centre, University of Bristol, Bristol.

ROSS, C.K., LAVIGNE, J., HAYFORD, J., BERRY, S., SINACORE, J. and PACHMAN, L. (1993) 'Psychological factors affecting reported pain in juvenile rheumatoid arthritis', *Journal of Pediatric Psychology*, 18, 561-573.

ROSS, D.M. and ROSS, S.A. (1984) 'The importance of the type of question, psychological climate and subject set in interviewing children about pain', *Pain*, 19, 71-79.

ROTHERAM-BORUS, M.J. and KOOPMAN, C. (1994) 'Protecting children's rights in AIDS research', in STANLEY, B. and SIBER, J.E. (eds) *Social Research on Children and Adolescents*, Newbury Park, California: Sage.

RUBENSTEIN, J., FELDMAN, S., RUBIN, C. and NOVECK, I. (1987) 'A cross-cultural comparison of children's drawings of same and mixed-sex peer interaction', *Journal of Cross-Cultural Psychology*, 18, 234-250.

RUSSELL, P. (1995) *Positive Choices: services for children with disabilities living away from home*, Council for Disabled Children, London.

SHEINGOLD, K. and TENNEY, Y. (1982) 'Memory for a salient childhood event', in NEISSER, U. (ed) *Memory Observed*, San Francisco: W.H. Freeman and Co.

SILVERS, R. (1976) 'Discovering children's culture', *Interchange*, 6, 47-52.

SMETANA, J. (1983) 'Social-cognitive development: domain distinctions and coordinations', *Developmental Review*, 3, 131-147.

SPINETTA, J.J. and DEASY-SPINETTA, P. (1981) 'Talking with children who have a life-threatening illness', in SPINETTA, J.J. and DEASY-SPINETTA, P. (eds) *Living with Childhood Cancer*, St Louis, Missouri: The C V Mosby Company.

STANLEY, B. and SIEBER, J.E. (1992) 'The ethics of social research on children and adolescents', in STANLEY, B. and SEIBER, J. (eds) *Social Research on Children and Adolescents: ethical issues*, Newbury Park, California: Sage.

STEVENSON-HINDE, J. and SHOULDICE, A. (1995) '4.5 to 7 years: fearful behaviour, fears and worries', *Journal of Child Psychology and Psychiatry*, 36, 6, 1027-1038.

STEWARD, M.S., BUSSEY, K., GOODMAN, G.S. and SAYWITZ, K.J. (1993) 'Implications of developmental research for interviewing children', *Child Abuse and Neglect*, 17, 1, 25-37.

STEWIG, J.W. (1994) 'First graders talk about paintings', *Journal of Educational Research*, 87, 5, 309-316.

TACKETT, P., KERR, N. and HELMSTADER, G. (1990) 'Stresses as perceived by children with physical disabilities and their mothers', *Journal of Rehabilitation*, 56, 3, 30-34.

TAMM, M.A. and GRANQVIST, A. (1995) 'The meaning of death for children and adolescents: a phenomenographic study of drawings', *Death Studies*, 19, 3, 203-222.

TAMMIVAARA, J. and ENRIGHT, S. (1986) 'On eliciting information: dialogues with child informants', *Anthropology and Education Quarterly*, 17, 218-238.

TARNOW, J. and GUTSTEIN, S. (1983) 'Children's preparatory behaviour for elective surgery', *Journal of the American Academy of Child Psychiatry*, 22, 365-369.

TELFAIR, J., MYERS, J. and DREZNER, S. (1994) 'Transfer as a component of the transition of adolescents with sickle cell disease to adult care: adolescent, adult and parent perspectives', *Journal of Adolescent Health*, 15, 7, 558-565.

THOMPSON, R.A. (1990) 'Vulnerability in research: a developmental perspective on research risk', *Child Development*, 61, 1-16.

THOMPSON, R.A. (1992) 'Developmental changes in research and risk benefit', in STANLEY, B. and SIEBER, J.E. (eds) *Social Research on Children and Adolescents*, Newbury Park, California: Sage.

TITTERTON, M. (1992) 'Managing threats to social welfare: the search for a new paradigm of welfare', *Journal of Social Policy*, 21,1, 1-23.

TOZER, R. and THORNTON, P. (1995) *A Meeting of Minds: older people as research advisers*, Social Policy

Reports Number Three, York: Social Policy Research Unit, University of York.

TYMCHUK, A.J. (1994) 'Assent processes', in STANLEY, B. and SIEBER, J.E. (eds) *Social Research on Children and Adolescents*, Newbury Park, California: Sage.

WADE, B. and MOORE, M. (1993) *Experiencing Special Education: what young people with special education needs can tell us*, Buckingham: Open University Press.

WAKSLER, F. (1986) 'Studying children: phenomenological insights', *Human Studies*, 9, 71-82.

WARD, L. (forthcoming 1997) *Seen and Heard: involving disabled children and young people in research and development projects*, York: Joseph Rowntree Foundation.

WELSH, I., FLANNIGAN, M. and RAVE, E. (1971) 'Children's drawings: what they tell us about the way kids see schools', *Innovator*, 2, 28-29.

WENESTAM, C. and WASS, H. (1987) 'Swedish and US children's thinking about death: a qualitative study and cross-cultural comparison', *Death Studies*, 11, 99-121.

WEST, A. and SAMMONS, P. (1991) *The Measurement of Children's Attitudes Towards School: the use of the Smiley' Scale*, Centre for Educational Research, London: London School of Economics and Political Science.

WILLIAMSON, H. and BUTLER, I. (1994) 'Children speak: perspectives on their social worlds', in BRANNEN, J. and O'BRIEN, M (eds) *Childhood and*

Parenthood: proceedings of the International Sociological Association Committee for Family Research Conference, London: Institute of Education, University of London.

WOODHEAD, M. (1990) 'Psychology and the cultural construction of children's needs', in JAMES, A. and PROUT, A. (eds) *Constructing and Reconstructing Childhood: contemporary issues in the sociological study of childhood*, London: The Falmer Press.

ZARB, G. (1992) 'On the road to Damascus: first steps towards changing the relations of disability research production', *Disability, Handicap and Society*, 7, 2, 125-138.

Index